CAPTURED
HISTORY

MAN ON THE MOON

HOW A PHOTOGRAPH MADE ANYTHING SEEM POSSIBLE

by Pamela Dell

Content Adviser: James Gerard, NASA Education Specialist,
Kennedy Space Center

Reading Adviser: Alexa L. Sandmann, EdD, Professor of Literacy,
College and Graduate School of Education, Health, and Human
Services, Kent State University

COMPASS POINT BOOKS

Compass Point Books
1710 Roe Crest Drive
North Mankato, MN 56003

Editor: Jennifer Fretland VanVoorst
Designer: Tracy Davies
Media Researcher: Svetlana Zhurkin
Library Consultant: Kathleen Baxter
Production Specialist: Sarah Bennett

Image Credits
Alamy/RIA Novosti, 18; Getty Images: CBS Photo Archive, 40, Chip Somodevilla,
46–47, *Evening Standard*, 39, Popperfoto, 9, Time & Life Pictures/NASA, 43;
iStockphoto/Florea Marius Catalin, 23; Mike Stimpson, 45; NASA: cover, 5, 7,
8, 10 (all), 12, 13, 15, 21, 22, 28, 30, 31, 33, 34, 37 (all), 41, 49, 50, 53, 55, 56
(bottom, all), 58 (all), 59 (all), Johnson Space Center, 26, 52, 57 (bottom), JPL,
20, 57 (top), Kennedy Space Center, 25; Wikipedia/NASA, 17, 56 (top).

This book was manufactured with paper containing
at least 10 percent post-consumer waste.

Library of Congress Cataloging-in-Publication Data
Dell, Pamela.
  Man on the moon: how a photograph made anything seem possible / by Pamela Dell.
      p. cm. — (Captured history)
  Includes bibliographical references and index.
  Summary: "Explores and analyzes the historical context and significance of Neil
Armstrong's iconic photograph of Buzz Aldrin"—Provided by publisher.
  ISBN 978-0-7565-4396-9 (library binding)
  ISBN 978-0-7565-4447-8 (paperback)
  1. Project Apollo (U.S.)—Juvenile literature. 2. Space flight to the moon—History—
20th century—Juvenile literature. 3. Photography—Influence—Juvenile literature.
I. Title. II. Series.
  TL789.8.U6A5324 2011
  629.45'4—dc22   2010038577

Visit Compass Point Books on the Internet at *www.capstonepub.com*

Printed in the United States of America in North Mankato, Minnesota.
052013   007328R

TABLEOFCONTENTS

ChapterOne
FANTASTIC VOYAGE

Descending swiftly toward the moon in their lunar module, called *Eagle*, the two astronauts had their hands full. For one thing, their spacecraft had only about 80 seconds of fuel left in its descent tank. If the fuel ran out, the entire mission would have to be abruptly aborted—a disappointing and dangerous prospect.

In addition, landing was looking like a big challenge. *Eagle*'s computer was overloaded and was triggering one frightening alarm after another. With less power than today's typical desktop calculator, it could not keep up with all the calculations it was supposed to be making. And when the vehicle's commander, astronaut Neil Armstrong, finally had a chance to look out one of *Eagle*'s windows, he did not like what he saw.

It appeared that the craft had overshot the planned touchdown area. Now the automatic piloting system had locked onto a new landing site, and it couldn't have been a much worse spot. *Eagle* was heading directly into an area strewn with boulders that Armstrong later described as "the size of Volkswagens." Worse, the boulder field was along the edge of a crater the size of a football field.

Armstrong and his Apollo 11 crewmate, Edwin E. "Buzz" Aldrin Jr., knew it was time to take matters into their own hands. It would be impossible to land safely on the treacherous terrain they were heading for. To set down on

Astronaut Michael Collins, who remained in the command module, photographed *Eagle* as it descended to the moon's surface.

the lunar surface in one piece, they clearly could not use the autopilot. They would have to recalculate their position and manually guide *Eagle* to a safe landing.

While Aldrin shouted out numbers showing their decreasing altitude and speed, Armstrong slowly and carefully steered *Eagle* to a better landing site. The slowness of the descent was agonizing to the Mission Control scientists on Earth. Besides all the other dangers, they were quite aware of the vehicle's nearly empty fuel tank.

Armstrong aimed for a fairly smooth area beyond the crater field. He planned to land just in front of the terminator, the edge of the moon's dark shadow. Before landing, the astronauts rolled the lunar module so they were seated face-up inside. This allowed *Eagle*'s landing radar to determine the craft's altitude and lock on the moon's surface. Landing properly was critical. If the vehicle's landing gear accidentally struck the surface, very serious problems could arise. The worst would be toppling over. That would make it impossible for the astronauts to leave the moon.

But there was more trouble to come. In its final stage of descent, the vehicle was suddenly enveloped in a thick cloud of moon dust, kicked up by the lunar module's exhaust system. Visibility was so poor that it was almost impossible to tell how close the moon's surface was. Nevertheless, with just 20 seconds of fuel left, the spacecraft set down without a hitch. It landed in a place called the Sea of Tranquility. When the engine was shut off, the dust immediately settled, clearing the view. Beyond *Eagle*'s windows lay the barren surface of an alien world.

Immediately Armstrong reported back to Mission Control

As *Eagle* landed, it cast a shadow on the moon's surface.

in Houston, Texas. What he said has echoed through history: "The Eagle has landed." In Houston, the ground controller quickly replied, using the code name for the now landed lunar module: "Roger, Tranquility. We copy you on the ground. You've got a bunch of guys about to turn blue. We're breathing again."

It was 4:18 p.m. Eastern time on July 20, 1969. It had been only four days since Apollo 11's liftoff from Earth.

DAILY EXPRESS

No. 21,499 MONDAY JULY 21 1969 Weather: Mainly cloudy. Price 5d.

Man is on the moon...

THE EAGLE HAS LANDED

ALDRIN ... They were bang on time

ARMSTRONG—landed the moon module

MAN landed safely on the moon at 9.18 (British time) last night–July 20, 1969.

The space ferry Eagle with Neil Armstrong and Edwin Aldrin on board planted its four, dish-like feet on a site surrounded by a sea of dead lava.

The historic touchdown message said: "Tranquility base, The Eagle has landed."

Then Armstrong said after landing: "We are breathing again. Thanks a lot."

A message sent to Michael Collins in command ship Columbia, orbiting the moon, said: "Eagle at Tranquillity." Collins replied: "I heard the whole thing. Good show."

The crew began checking the angle of the spacecraft on the moon—vital for a successful return to Columbia.

The time of the journey from take-off from earth to landing on the moon was given as 102 hours 45 minutes 42 seconds. The original flight plan gave the time as 102 hours 51 minutes.

Armstrong reported: "WE ARE IN FOOTBALL PITCH-SIZED CRATER. IT LOOKS BEAUTIFUL FROM HERE, TRANQUILLITY."

When all measures to ensure safe take-off back

ROBIN ESSER, ROSS MARK and RICHARD KILIAN, Houston, Texas.

to Columbia were completed, the plan was for Armstrong and Aldrin to sleep in readiness for their moon walk this morning.

Ten minutes after landing Aldrin radioed: "We'll get to the details of what's around here. But it looks like a collection of every variety of shape, angularity, granularity, a collection of just about every kind of rock.

"Colour depends on what angle you're looking at ... rocks and boulders look as though they're going to have some interesting colours."

The initial report said Eagle was at an angle of 4½ degrees, well inside the range for take-off again.

Later, Armstrong was able to report that he had no trouble going from a weightless condition to the one-sixth gravity of the moon. "It's just like an airplane," he said.

The build-up to the dramatic touchdown had gone like this (B.S.T. times):

2.22 p.m. Edwin Aldrin moved out of the command module into Eagle, the moon-landing craft. There had been an anxious moment coming back from the back of the moon when radio communication was exceptionally bad. But soon flight control at Houston was reporting "all systems operating just fine."

3.23 p.m. Mission Commander Armstrong joined Aldrin in the lunar module to help prepare it for undocking from the mother-ship.

Armstrong, Aldrin and Collins had all slept calmly and soundly for nearly six hours before starting the final manoeuvres.

When mission control woke them with a cheery "Apollo 11! Apollo 11, good morning," a lazy voice drifted back from the moon: "Oh my, you guys wake up early."

Mission control: "Yes, you're two minutes early

on the wakeup. Looks like you were really sawing them away."

Spaceship: "You're right."

Mission control reported that they had been closely monitoring the spaceship as the men slept, and it was in good order for the great day. Armstrong replied: "We sure appreciate that because I sure haven't been watching."

Mike Collins was last off, to sleep and flight surgeon Ken Beers rejoiced: "They are really playing it cool. Their pulse rate sank to about 40 and they did not toss and turn."

6.47 p.m. Armstrong and Aldrin were given the go-ahead to undock their fragile moon-landing craft from the mother-ship. This was only five minutes before the craft passed behind the moon and radio contact was temporarily lost.

On a signal from control at Houston the two moon-walkers had undocked their landing craft from Columbia, and left the command module in orbit about 60 miles above the moon with Michael Collins at the controls.

The signal from Houston said: "You have the GO for undocking." Armstrong replied calmly: "Roger ... understand."

The 12 latches which held Eagle and the command craft together were released by Michael Collins. The two craft continued in convoy round the moon for 35 minutes. Armstrong and Aldrin made ready for the descent in their silver, black and gold Eagle.

Armstrong called with his first trace of exultation: "EAGLE UNDOCKED .. EAGLE HAS WINGS."

Collins said: "Looks like you've got a mighty good flying machine, Eagle, despite the fact you're upside down."

In the separation manoeuvre Armstrong and Aldrin had to rotate Eagle 180 degrees so that its main rocket engine pointed in the direction they wished to go.

Twenty-five minutes later, with the two ships 40 feet apart, Collins triggered his main rocket motor and shot nearly two miles ahead of the moon-lander. He called: "SEE YOU LATER."

Rolling

Aldrin radioed to Collins: "You're going right down U.S. One, Mike." The astronauts had nick-named part of their route after the main highway which runs down the East coast of the United States.

The "Go" decision to start this first stage of descent was given by flight director Gene Kranz: "Eagle—this is Houston. You are go for D.O.I." (Descent Orbit Insertion) Aldrin replied: "Houston, this is Eagle Go for D.O.I."

Nine miles above the moon—the nearest point to which man had previously dared venture—a signal from Houston, told them: "You are for PDI." This initial stand for Powered Descent Initiation.

They fired their rocket engine again and started gliding down, aiming for a landing on a plateau measuring eight miles by four in the south-east corner of the so-called Sea of Tranquility.

One of the men in charge of communications asked the spacemen to watch out for a lovely girl with a big Chinese rabbit who had been banished to the moon, according to legend, 4,000 years ago. One of the spacemen replied: "We'll keep close watch for the bunny girl."

At 7,600ft., a point known in the flight plan as the High-Gate, Armstrong and Aldrin were standing upright in safety harness, one on each side of the control panel in their cabin, the size of two telephone kiosks placed side by side.

At 500ft., the Low-Gate point, with half a mile to go, their rockets brakes had slowed them to a mere mile a minute.

When the round landing feet were precisely 8ft. 8in. above the moon, first contact with it was made by rapier-like steel probes projecting downwards through three of the feet.

A warning light flashed in the cabin. Armstrong paused a second, as it was planned he should do, and shut off the engine. Eagle bumped, bounced and settled. Man had made his first landfall outside his native earth.

APOLLO 11 MOON LANDING SITE

LUNA 15 DIPS, THEN GOES 'OUT OF RANGE'

Express Staff Reporter

THE RUSSIANS reported last night that its unmanned and mysterious Luna 15 had changed orbit near moon space, bringing it within 10 miles of the moon's surface.

It was "continuing scientific exploration of near moon space" said the Soviet News Agency.

Disappeared

Western observers took the view that the last possibility that Luna 15 would forestall Apollo 11 in landing on the moon to collect the samples disappeared just after eight o'clock last night.

Because then, the moon disappeared below the horizon of the vast space communications centre from which the Russians have been transmitting its control messages.

No more control could presumably be carried out until the moon rose again.

The front page of the *Daily Express* in London, England, gave a timeline of the historic moon landing.

A HISTORIC SPACE MISSION

Astronauts (from left) Neil Armstrong, Michael Collins, and Buzz Aldrin formed the crew of Apollo 11.

The three-man Apollo 11 crew blasted off from Cape Kennedy, Florida, at 9:32 a.m. Eastern time on July 16, 1969. After the spacecraft had orbited Earth one and a half times, the engines of the Saturn V rocket that had launched it into space fired again. This shot the two-part spacecraft out of Earth's orbit and on its way to the moon, a journey of more than 235,000 miles (378,196 kilometers). The astronauts, Neil Armstrong, Buzz Aldrin, and Michael Collins, rode in the command module, called *Columbia*. Attached to it was *Eagle*, the lunar module that would land on the moon.

When the two-part spacecraft was free of Earth's gravity, a tricky move had to be made. Thousands of miles out in space, the two modules separated. After disconnecting, *Columbia* turned around and connected with *Eagle* nose to nose. The Saturn V rocket was allowed to float off into space. Then the historic journey continued.

By July 19 *Columbia* and *Eagle* had entered the moon's orbit. On the dark side of the moon and temporarily out of contact with Earth, the crew split up. Armstrong and Aldrin climbed through a hatch from *Columbia* into *Eagle*. The two spacecraft then disengaged again. *Columbia* moved away from *Eagle* at 120 feet (37 meters) per minute. They had to separate quickly so each vehicle's guidance system could work without interference from the other.

Collins, alone in the command module, continued to orbit the moon. *Eagle*, however, was taking another course. Returning to the moon's Earth-facing side, it regained contact with Mission Control. Armstrong and Aldrin were ready to begin their historic journey as the first humans to venture onto the lunar surface.

Onto the Moon

Aldrin and Armstrong had managed to successfully land *Eagle* on the moon. But they had a lot to do before they could leave the spacecraft. They stayed in the vehicle more than six hours after landing. Most of their time was spent going over checklists and taking care of many important technical tasks. They also put on their spacesuits, which were designed to help them work safely and comfortably in the vacuum of space.

Finally Armstrong left *Eagle*. On the way down a ladder attached to the landing gear, he pulled a cord that caused an onboard TV camera to begin recording him. As the camera rolled, Armstrong cautiously descended. The bottom step of the ladder was three and a half feet (1 meter) above the moon's surface. Armstrong was concerned about losing his balance and falling in his big, bulky spacesuit. If the suit were to be torn or punctured, he would die in less than a minute.

SUITING UP

The lack of atmosphere on the moon means that there is no oxygen for astronauts to breathe. It also means that there is no blanket of gases to trap or deflect the sun's rays. Temperatures on the moon range from -387 degrees Fahrenheit (-233 degrees Celsius) at night to 253° F (123° C) during the day. A lot went into creating a spacesuit that would protect an astronaut in these extreme conditions.

Despite its many layers, the spacesuit designed for the Apollo 11 mission weighed a relatively light 180 pounds (82 kg)—but only 30 pounds (14 kg) on the moon—including the backpack, which held a Portable Life Support System. Today's space shuttle spacesuits weigh about 310 pounds (141 kg), but in orbit, where there is no gravity, they weigh nothing.

But because the moon's gravity is 83 percent less than that of Earth, things drop much more slowly, so that step was not difficult. Armstrong stepped onto the moon's surface, the first human to do so.

With the world watching the live television broadcast, Armstrong spoke a few now-historic words. He said, "That's one small step for a man, one giant leap for mankind." To many people watching, it sounded as if he had said, "One small step for man, one giant leap for mankind," since the "a" ran into the word "man." But no matter what one heard, the message was clear: A monumental achievement had occurred.

"That's one small step for a man, one giant leap for mankind."

Buzz Aldrin followed Armstrong onto the lunar surface.

At Mission Control in Houston, Texas, flight controllers watched grainy footage of the mission on their computer monitors as well as a large TV screen.

Iconic Images

Although live video of the first walk on the moon was being televised on Earth, Armstrong and Aldrin also had small regular film cameras to capture their experience in photographs. Among the many images from the historic event, one picture of Aldrin stood out. It was an image that would itself rocket around the globe, electrifying the world's imagination.

Photography is a powerful medium. Since the time of the earliest human beings, people's minds have been struck by the power of certain real-life scenes. Through the ages art in various forms has re-created such scenes. But only through the use of cameras can moments be frozen in time, without re-creation, to be viewed long after the moment they occurred.

Every photograph depicts a single moment, of course. But in some of those single moments a whole story can be found. In some cases the image of the moment caught on film can represent much more than simply what's going on in the picture. This was certainly the case with the image of Aldrin on the moon. It showed a bizarre-looking figure, suited up for space and standing in a shallow crater. Behind him the black sky and the rocky, desolate landscape emphasized the stark strangeness of his location. But this photo was not just an image of someone named Buzz Aldrin wearing a spacesuit. To people in every country on Earth, it represented—and still represents—much more.

Here was a man who was more than 235,000 miles (378,196 kilometers) from our planet. He and one other crew member had reached another world. It was a photograph that told many stories, an image with various possible meanings. The most obvious was, of course, how far—both literally and figuratively—the human race had come since its beginnings. The photograph also gave people hope for the future. If human beings could land on the moon, then surely anything was possible. For some, though, the most important meaning of the photograph was that the man in the picture came from the United States.

Life magazine chose Neil Armstrong's photograph of Buzz Aldrin on the moon as one of the 100 photographs that changed the world.

ChapterTwo
THE GREAT SPACE RACE

Had the president lost his mind? Many people had to wonder when President John F. Kennedy spoke to Congress on May 25, 1961. "I believe this nation," he said, "should commit itself to achieving the goal, before this decade is out, of landing a man on the moon and returning him safely to the Earth."

Some Americans thought the president's idea was the most unrealistic thing they'd ever heard. But others believed it was possible and strongly wanted to see it happen. Four years earlier the Soviet Union had caught the United States by surprise with its own space success story.

A Rivalry Is Born

The event that took America by surprise occurred October 4, 1957. That day the Soviets launched a satellite into space. Called *Sputnik 1*, it was the first artificial satellite to orbit Earth. The beach-ball-sized object circled the globe once, a journey that took only 96 minutes.

Just one month later, *Sputnik 2* followed *Sputnik 1* into space. This was an even more impressive feat. *Sputnik 2* carried much heavier cargo—including Laika, a very-much-alive dog. The two successful spacecraft launches brought pride to the Soviet Union. Premier Nikita Khrushchev boasted, as one Kennedy biographer put it, about "another Communist triumph over a decaying capitalistic system."

"I believe this nation should commit itself to achieving the goal ... of landing a man on the moon and returning him safely to the Earth."

A replica of *Sputnik 1*

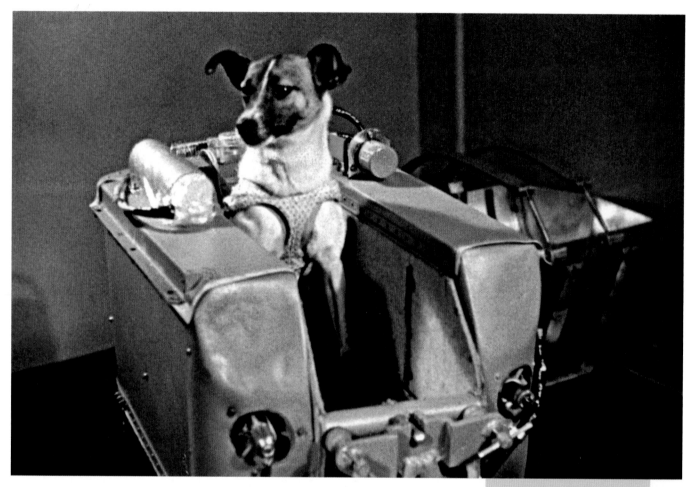

In July 1955, two years before the Soviet satellite launches, the American government had announced plans for a similar mission. By 1957 the goal was near. But with the successful Sputnik missions, the Soviet Union had beaten the United States to the accomplishment—and with larger, better satellites than the one the U.S. was building. News of the two Sputnik voyages awed people around the world. But in America, it came as a shock—and sparked an international rivalry.

The Soviet Union was a large, powerful Communist

country. That made it America's biggest enemy. Further, the United States prided itself on its technological know-how. With the Sputnik launches, it had suddenly been shown up as "second best." But this was the least of America's worries. Many citizens feared the Soviets now could launch weapon-carrying missiles at the United States.

The desire to outdo the Soviet Union energized the nation. Americans wanted to see their country achieve bigger and better things in space—and to do them first. To many people, beating the Soviet Union also would symbolize the superiority of democracy over communism. The Sputnik launches accelerated the U.S. space program. What came to be called the space race was on.

Launching the U.S. Space Program

On January 31, 1958, just a few months after the two Sputnik flights, the United States launched its first satellite, *Explorer 1*, into orbit. This satellite carried scientific instruments for conducting experiments in space. It was the first of a series of Explorer spacecraft that carried out many important scientific studies.

The Soviets' Sputnik successes also led the U.S. Congress to establish a major branch of the government devoted to space exploration. This department, known as the National Aeronautics and Space Administration (NASA), has overseen America's prestigious space programs since it was created on October 1, 1958.

The United States didn't pull ahead immediately in the

space race, however. An even bigger embarrassment than the Sputnik launches was to come. By early 1961 NASA was preparing to send a man into space for the first time. But again the Soviets beat the U.S. to the punch. On April 12, 1961, a 27-year-old Soviet fighter pilot, Yuri Gagarin, blasted off alone in a small space capsule. It was the world's first piloted space mission. Like *Sputnik 1* Gagarin's spacecraft circled Earth once. The orbit lasted just 108 minutes.

Less than a month after Gagarin's flight, on May 7,

U.S. newspapers reported the achievement of Gagarin's flight while acknowledging that the country was losing ground in the space race.

American astronaut Alan Shepard followed him into space. Though this was the first manned American space mission, Shepard's flight was not as spectacular as Gagarin's. Shepard's spacecraft never orbited Earth. It simply took a 15-minute flight 116 miles (187 km) up into the atmosphere and returned.

The Soviets' seemingly huge victory in the space race added to the impression that they were light years ahead. But Shepard's successful flight created a frenzy of excitement among Americans. Knowing that the American public was now enthusiastically behind the space race, President

U.S. President John F. Kennedy congratulated astronaut Alan Shepard on becoming the first American in space.

WHAT THE SOVIETS DIDN'T TELL

A 1964 Soviet stamp depicted early satellites, including Sputnik 1 *(left).*

Though the Soviet Union was proud and public about its accomplishments in space, it was deeply secretive about its failures and disasters. During the Cold War years, when the United States and the Soviet Union were the bitterest of rivals, many rumors swirled about Soviet space tragedies. Most were simply myths or hearsay. Others were an unreliable mix of fact and fiction. But a few were true, and the facts only came to public awareness years later, after the fall of the Soviet Union. Here are a few Soviet space disasters:

- October 24, 1960: A massive fire broke out on the launch pad at what is now Baikonur Cosmodrome, destroying a huge Soviet R-16 nuclear missile. The horrific disaster, which occurred moments before a test launch of the missile, claimed about 125 lives, including that of the commander responsible for overseeing the countdown. The event was hidden—even from families of the dead—until the 1990s.
- March 23, 1961: Twenty-four-year-old cosmonaut Valentin Bondarenko was killed during a training mission on the ground. When the pressurized space chamber he was seated in burst into flame, the intense pressure kept him from getting out. According to a statement published in a Soviet journal, "Prior to 1986 no Soviet book or magazine had ever mentioned the existence of a cosmonaut named Valentin Bondarenko."
- April 24, 1967: The mechanically troubled spacecraft *Soyuz 1* crash-landed in a field after having what the Soviets described as problems with the parachute system. The one cosmonaut aboard, Vladimir Komarov, became the first person known to be killed in a spaceflight.
- June 29, 1971: All three *Soyuz 11* cosmonauts were found dead when their spacecraft returned to Earth. They were killed when a malfunctioning pressure valve kept them from getting air.
- September 13, 2001: A story in the Russian news media claimed that the Soviets had launched three manned space vehicles before Gagarin went up—in 1957, 1958, and 1959. The report came from Mikhail Rudenko, who worked as a Soviet space engineer during those years. Rudenko said all three cosmonauts, whose names he gave, had lost their lives in flight, but that the Soviets had hidden the information. Is Rudenko's story fact or fiction? No one has proved or disproved his claim.

Kennedy acted quickly. He consulted with top experts in the space program and with Vice President Lyndon B. Johnson. He pressured experts to come up with a space program that could be successfully accomplished before the Soviets could manage the same thing. After careful consideration of all the possibilities, one option stood out. Sending men to the moon, the experts agreed, was the way to go.

Steps to the Moon

With the goal determined, Kennedy's speech to Congress in May 1961 was a call to action. He began pushing NASA scientists to make a moon landing happen before the end of the 1960s. This was a tall order. NASA had less than nine years to hit the mark.

To some, the president's goal seemed too ambitious, even ridiculous, considering how little the United States had accomplished so far. American spacecraft had spent a grand total of 15 minutes in space. No astronaut had walked in space or even been shot into orbit.

The goal of reaching the moon was announced only after careful consideration of many factors. The mission would require enormous technological advancements. It also would cost a huge amount of money. The public would have to strongly support the idea to make it doable.

Kennedy's address enlivened the public imagination. From then on, a series of major NASA missions were carried out. Behind each of these programs—Mercury, then Gemini, and finally the Apollo missions to the moon—lay the president's vision when he had called the country to the challenge.

In the next half decade there were technological advances on a historic scale. The main purpose of the Mercury program was to increase technological understanding and experience. Another purpose was to learn more about how spaceflight affects human beings. The Gemini program was the connecting link between the Mercury and Apollo missions. Whereas Mercury was primarily exploratory and experimental, the Apollo program's mission was to actually get astronauts to the moon. Gemini's purpose was to demonstrate successfully all the skills needed for people to make that journey into space.

In 1962, as part of the Mercury 6 program, John Glenn became the first American to orbit Earth.

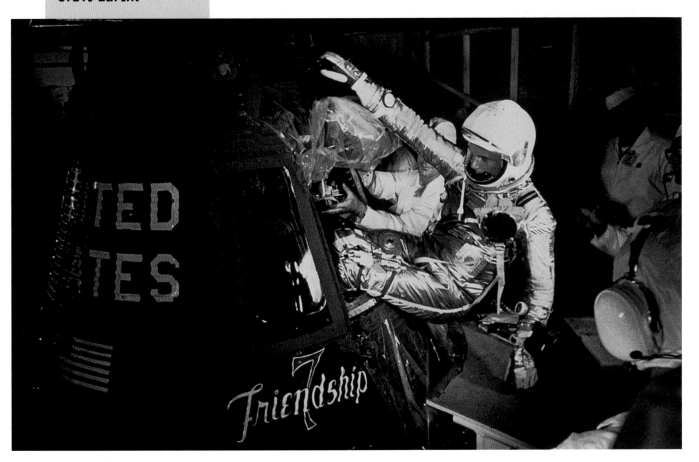

NASA moved quickly. First many unmanned test maneuvers took place. An important reason for these crewless flights was to check various systems on the powerful Saturn rocket that would launch the Apollo vehicles into

In 1965 Gemini 4 astronaut Edward White became the first American to leave his spacecraft and float in the vacuum of space.

space. Later unmanned flights tested the command and lunar modules and many complicated systems that would make human travel to the moon a safe possibility.

From Tragedy to Stunning Success

The race to the moon was bustling along. But on the evening of January 27, 1969, the first manned Apollo mission ended in tragedy. Apollo 1, also known as mission AS-204, was scheduled to take three astronauts into space. Lieutenant Colonel Virgil "Gus" Grissom, Lieutenant Colonel Edward White, and Lieutenant Commander Roger Chaffee were sealed inside the command module atop the massive Saturn launch rocket. Their mission was a launch pad test of the Apollo/Saturn space vehicle. But before the countdown could begin, a flash fire broke out in the command module. It spread quickly.

A wall of flame and intense pressure trapped the astronauts in the command module. The vehicle had no quick-escape hatch, nor had it been equipped with fire extinguishers. Extreme heat, explosions caused by pressure, and the escape of poisonous carbon monoxide gas delayed rescue efforts. By the time the hatch was opened, only five minutes after the astronauts reported the fire, all three had died. The command module was a severely burned and blasted out hunk of metal.

After the disastrous end to the first Apollo mission, new safety features were put into Apollo spacecraft, and the program had no further casualties.

Over the next four years, another 11 Apollo missions took place. The fifth of these was the July 1969 first-ever moon landing of Apollo 11. Later Apollo missions landed spacecraft on the moon as well. Only Apollo 13 had any trouble. Its moon landing was aborted before touchdown after an explosion occurred in the vehicle's service module. At the time of the accident, the crew was about 200,000 miles (321,869 km) from Earth. But they managed to return home safely. The Apollo program concluded in 1975, having made six successful moon landings. President Kennedy's dream of the United States' winning the space race had been triumphantly realized.

Astronauts (from left) Edward White, Gus Grissom, and Roger Chaffee died inside the Apollo 1 command module.

ChapterThree
MAN IN A MOON SUIT

After the success of the Apollo 11 mission, news of "men on the moon" flew around planet Earth, causing celebration, envy, and, in some cases, doubt. Skeptics wondered whether such a seemingly impossible feat had really happened.

The mission's many photographs and film footage confirm that the impossible had, in fact, been accomplished. Only 15 minutes after Armstrong stepped down from *Eagle*, Aldrin followed him to the moon's surface. One of the astronauts' first moves was to plant an American flag in the ground. There has hardly ever been a better photo opportunity, and the camera mounted on *Eagle* captured Armstrong and Aldrin planting the flag. The astronauts also documented their work using a handheld camera.

Famous Photo

The two-man crew had a lot to do on the moon's surface and only a short scheduled time to do it in. They set up scientific experiments near Tranquility Base, the name given to *Eagle*'s landing spot. They also collected rocks and other geological samples. Altogether they gathered 47.5 pounds (21.5 kilograms) of moon material to bring home. As the TV camera automatically panned the area and tracked their movements, the astronauts took dozens of pictures with their still camera. Armstrong shot most of them. After taking about 50 pictures, he captured the iconic moment.

RAISING THE FLAG

Neil Armstrong and Buzz Aldrin were photographed planting the U.S. flag on the lunar surface.

A lot went into the matter of taking an American flag to the moon—and leaving it lodged in the ground there. A lot of thought. A lot of engineering. A lot of trial and error. And a lot of controversy. The act was controversial because some people were very much against the idea of a single nation's embedding its own flag in moon rock.

According to the United Nations' Outer Space Treaty, "outer space, including the moon and other celestial bodies, is not subject to national appropriation by claim of sovereignty, by means of occupation, or by any other means."

Some felt that raising an American flag on the moon was a clear, and offensive, signal of possession. The United States had signed the Outer Space Treaty too, which meant it could not claim any part of the moon as American territory.

Scores of people wrote the United Nations suggesting other flags they thought should also be planted on the moon, including the flag of the United Nations. But the U.S. Congress had approved funding for the Apollo 11 mission, and the government insisted on the U.S. flag and only the U.S. flag.

Congress also made it clear that leaving a U.S. flag on the moon did not mean the United States was claiming it. "This act," a congressional resolution said, "is intended as a symbolic gesture of national pride in achievement." The intent was simply to mark an accomplishment, like placing a flag on the peak of a mountain you have climbed. Later Buzz Aldrin told a reporter that when he looked at the flag after they had erected it, he sensed a "mystical unification of all people in the world."

Although the American flag was the only flag to be planted in lunar soil, it wasn't the only flag to go to the moon. The Apollo 11 astronauts carried miniature flags from every American state and from all the countries that belonged to the United Nations. They brought flags of some nonmember countries as well. When they returned home, they presented the flags to the state governors and to the leaders of the other countries.

This photograph, of Aldrin standing a few paces beyond the lunar module, soon took on a remarkable life of its own. Here was a faceless creature, a spaceman seemingly straight out of science fiction, standing in utter isolation. Below him is only barren, rocky ground. Behind him, the sky is black. His bulky white spacesuit is covered with tubes and knobs, and he wears a large white backpack. His left arm is raised and bent, as if he might be about to reach for something or

wave hello. (He was actually looking at a checklist printed on his sleeve.)

Aldrin, in the photo, is an anonymous figure in an alien landscape—but wait. Look closer! On the astronaut's left shoulder is a bright patch of color that cannot be missed. It's a red, white, and blue emblem that stands out with high visibility in this strange, colorless world. That emblem is the flag of the United States of America. This is indeed part of this famous photograph's significance.

A Story in Pictures

Something else is interesting about this now-legendary photo. The faceless spaceman is not recognizable because of the shiny protective visor that covers his entire face. A closer look at the visor reveals more information. The scene captured in the reflection seems to give the shot its most spectacular quality.

Here the viewer sees a strange, futuristic scene: Aldrin's long, dark shadow in the foreground. A few flagged experiments the men had set up can be seen on the upper left side. And in the distance, standing beside the shining lunar module, we see another white-suited figure. It is Neil Armstrong, the photographer himself.

The TV camera was tracking the astronauts' movements, of course. But as Armstrong realized, using the reflected image in the visor was the only way the two astronauts could capture themselves together in a still photograph.

This famous image, now catalogued by NASA as photo

The reflection in Aldrin's visor captures both the photographer and the lunar module.

number AS11-40-5903, did not instantly show up in the press back home. On the day of the moonwalk, newspapers and magazines around the world were offered three images for publication. They could select a fuzzy image taken from the live television broadcast. They could use the official Apollo 11 crew photograph. It simply showed the three suited-up astronauts: Neil Armstrong, Buzz Aldrin, and

MADE FOR THE MOON

The astronauts captured a still image of a print one of their boots made in the loose lunar surface.

The first still camera used on the moon was a specially designed 500 EL model Hasselblad Data Camera. Everything about the camera's design had to follow strict NASA specifications to make it easy and safe to use in an environment extremely different from Earth's.

The camera was loaded with Kodak 70 millimeter film, which provided about 160 pictures per roll. It was attached to the astronaut's chest, but because of the spacesuit limitations, the camera was built without a viewfinder. Before embarking for the moon, the astronauts practiced shooting pictures without a viewfinder to make sure they knew what they were doing.

That little black Hasselblad sparked a trend that didn't fade for many years. Suddenly a camera had to be black to be considered a professional piece of equipment rather than something amateurish. Few non-black cameras were manufactured. It took decades before it was common for camera companies to offer models in silver and other colors.

Michael Collins, who, during the landing, had continued circling the moon in the command module. Or they could choose an artist's illustration of the extravehicular activity.

Accompanied by one, two, or all three of the pictures, the news was splashed across the front pages of most newspapers around the world. This was especially true in the United States, where the moon landing created widespread national pride.

In the Soviet Union, however, there was little pride in starting out strong in the space race only to come in a distant second in the biggest accomplishment so far. There the news was buried in the back pages of the papers. The Soviets quietly bowed out of the moon race.

Making a Good Photo Great

When the Buzz Aldrin image finally became available, it had the kind of dramatic quality editors crave. The photograph has vibrant color and clarity. It has a perfect exposure and is sharply focused, which is amazing considering Armstrong shot it without being able to look through a viewfinder.

Everyone agreed that the picture was good—but apparently some at NASA thought it could be made better. The original shot, initially labeled 69-HC-684, wasn't perfectly framed. Armstrong had failed to center his subject in the photo. Aldrin appeared so high in the shot that the very top of his head and backpack were cut off. There was a lot of moon surface compared with the human figure. Part of the lunar module was showing in the bottom right of the picture as well.

That's not the way things looked when the news media got hold of the photograph, however. Someone at NASA had done some work on the photo before it was released.

Anyone who compares the original and the press version of the photo can see the difference. The photo sent to journalists around the world is clearly darker than the original, with improved contrast between lights and darks. It shows more black sky above Aldrin's head than the original does. And the bottom and both sides of the shot have been cropped. The alterations darkened the distracting elements and centered the astronaut in the picture. The cropping gives the image more power because the spaceman is now the central focus of the picture.

In the altered version, the missing upper edge of Aldrin's life-support backpack is also filled in, though it was cut off in the original. In a time before photo-doctoring software, a NASA artist had made the changes by hand. Another thing a few sharp eyes caught was what was missing. The astronauts' spacesuits were equipped with a small vertical antenna rising from the top of the backpack. This antenna should have been clearly visible against the dark sky behind Aldrin. But look closely and you'll see it's not showing. This detail proves that one of the most famous photos in the world is not quite as it should be.

The original photograph taken by Neil Armstrong

The altered photograph that was released to the press

ChapterFour
A WORLDWIDE ICON

When Neil Armstrong stepped onto the surface of the moon, an estimated 528 million television viewers were tuned in worldwide. The planned extravehicular activity was scheduled for about 9 p.m. Eastern time. That meant the astronauts would be performing their lunar tasks during peak television viewing hours.

Mission Control told Armstrong and Aldrin, "You guys are getting prime time on TV there."

Referring to the video camera, one of the astronauts replied, "I hope that little TV set works. We'll see."

It was amazing that it did function, given the technology of the time and the distance between *Eagle*'s crew and those watching them on Earth. The camera weighed a scant seven pounds (3 kg), and most of its 250-plus parts were very small. Because of the shape of the camera, it had to be mounted upside down on the lunar module. So the footage of Armstrong descending the ladder and setting foot on the moon had to be inverted for broadcast on Earth.

A bit later the astronauts removed the camera, positioned it upright on a tripod, and set it up about 10 yards (9 meters) from their vehicle. It remained there for the rest of their mission. The live moonwalk footage that was broadcast was fuzzy. But viewers were thrilled anyway.

The day after the historic walk, newspapers around the

"I hope that little TV set works. We'll see."

The moon landing was broadcast on large screens in public places around the world, such as in London's Trafalgar Square.

world gave the story major coverage. But editors who wanted a real-time photograph had to use the blurry picture from the TV footage. It was as close as they could get to a dramatic visual image, so they took it.

VIDEO FOOTAGE DIFFICULTIES

Travelers at New York City's JFK International Airport gathered to watch the live broadcast from the moon.

What viewers saw on TV the night of July 20, 1969, might have been blurry, ghostly images of two spacemen rambling around the moon, but they were still thrilled. What they didn't realize, though, was that the quality of the footage that aired was much worse than what *Eagle*'s small video camera actually shot. The camera worked amazingly well, considering it had to function on the moon and send the video back hundreds of thousands of miles to Earth. The problem was that the camera was built to employ an unusual video format, one that TV cameras back home could not read.

Thus the footage had to be beamed instead to various tracking stations on Earth. These sites then had the job of converting it as well as possible to something readable by TV. Next they relayed the footage to Mission Control. From there it went out to the world via live TV. By the time it showed up on the TV screen, after this conversion process, the footage was seriously degraded—thus the blurry, fuzzy effect.

But considering that this was long before sophisticated digital technology, getting the moonwalk "show" on live TV at all was quite an impressive accomplishment. On a final not-so-great note, however, no one seems to have kept track of that original clear videotape. It's missing, and after years of searching, everyone's given up ever finding it.

Futuristic AS11-40-5903

Only days later NASA began offering something much better: photos taken by the astronauts themselves. They included the doctored picture that went down in history and that still serves as the primary symbol of the event—the

Neil Armstrong, who took most of the still photos during the mission, photographed Buzz Aldrin approaching the lunar module.

futuristic photo numbered AS11-40-5903 Neil Armstrong took of Buzz Aldrin.

The photo soon appeared in *Life* magazine. *Life* then had one of the largest U.S. magazine circulations. Its August 8, 1969, cover featured a black and white moonscape showing nothing but the rough lunar surface, a lot of footprints, and the American flag. The only text on the cover read simply "On the Moon: Footprints and Photographs by Neil Armstrong and Edwin Aldrin."

Inside the issue was a multipage photo spread. Its title was "Men on the Moon: Color Pictures of the Triumphant Apollo 11 Mission, Shot by the Astronauts on the Lunar Surface." The centerfold shot, a collector's item that wowed the readers, was the picture of Aldrin and his reflective visor. Beneath was the caption "A golden mirror for a moonscape."

Life published a special edition two days later. The issue, titled "To the Moon and Back," provided a pictorial history of the space race with details on both Soviet and American missions. On the cover was the moon-man image, enlarged and cropped to show only Aldrin's upper body, with the reflection standing out in clear detail. Already the photo was becoming an icon.

The same photo began showing up again and again on magazine covers and the front pages of newspapers around the world. In December 1969 the white-suited astronaut image appeared on the cover of *National Geographic*, along with the headline "First Explorers on the Moon." It was also on the front of a special moon issue of *Look* magazine, another major publication of the time.

SPECIAL EDITION

LIFE

TO THE MOON AND BACK

The cover of the August 10, 1969 special moon edition of *Life* magazine featured an enlarged and cropped version of the now-iconic photograph.

And this was just the beginning of the photo's life. It went on to appear in hundreds, if not thousands, of other publications and sometimes in surprising contexts. An unusual recent version was created by photographer Mike Stimpson. He reproduces well-known images using Legos. His collection, called "Classics in Lego," includes a photo of a single Lego figure wearing a helmet with a shiny visor and standing on a cratered surface. The photograph is captioned "Astronaut Buzz Aldrin on the surface of the moon in 1969."

I Want My MTV

Some news organizations chose a different photo to illustrate the moon landing. Some used a combination of images. But none of the images has quite equaled the Aldrin photo as a symbol of not only the Apollo 11 mission but also the whole moon-landing program. Still, a few of the other images have also gained a bit of iconic status over time. They include the shots of a bootprint deeply embedded in the lunar surface, Aldrin descending *Eagle*'s ladder, and Aldrin standing before the U.S. flag.

Like the famous moon-man photo, the flag image, especially, has also shown up in prominent places. It was seen by millions when it became a primary visual in the original MTV logo and a companion promotional video clip.

The Apollo 11 astronauts' feat, and the MTV clip, also inspired an awards show trophy. At its annual *MTV Video Music Awards*, the network gives winners statuettes of a shiny silver moon-man figure grasping an MTV flagpole.

Mike Stimpson attempted to replicate the famous photo of Buzz Aldrin using Legos.

Forty Years Later

Ask people today to describe the image that most fully captures the otherworldly strangeness of the first moon landing, and many will immediately mention the famous Buzz Aldrin photo. It has endured as an image that perfectly encapsulates the remarkable achievement. And in 2009 the photograph returned to the public eye on a widespread scale.

July 20, 2009, was the 40th anniversary of the Apollo 11 moonwalk. People around the world took time to reflect on the stunning human advancement represented by that feat. It was not celebrated as an American achievement so much as one, as Armstrong noted at the time, that belongs to all humankind.

Once again Apollo 11 images were everywhere. The most iconic photo was especially prominent, appearing in a wide range of media around the globe. In the United States, the picture appeared once again on front pages coast to coast. It showed up in newspapers ranging from the Pittsburgh *Tribune-Review* in Pennsylvania to the *Las Vegas Review-Journal* in Nevada, and from the Danbury, Connecticut, *News-Times* to the *Kansas City Star* in Missouri—and, as one writer put it, in a "bazillion" places in between.

The image was featured in commemorative Apollo 11 40th anniversary photomontages and in TV newscasts. But one of the more interesting ways it was used was in a Dover, Delaware, newspaper. The paper printed an entire page showing spacesuit technology, with the famous photo taking up more than half the page. The shot was used as a reference

Newspapers from the time of the Apollo 11 moon landing were on display at Kennedy Space Center in honor of the 40th anniversary of the historic event.

in explaining nine of the 21 layers of the Apollo 11 spacesuits.

Another indication of the photo's impact and powerful cultural importance came with the publication that year of *Moonfire*, a 40th anniversary, limited edition book about the Apollo 11 mission. With this single iconic image gracing its cover, the book has great dramatic appeal. *Moonfire* sold for $1,000.

Moon Landings Faked!

The ability to send men to the moon—and get them back—without a hitch is a huge technological feat, to say the least. It is not surprising, given its difficulty and complexity, that there are those who believe the whole venture was a giant hoax. There were skeptics when Armstrong and Aldrin showed up in those grainy television images. A Gallup survey in 1999 found that 6 percent of Americans were convinced that nobody had ever been to the moon. There are at least as many doubters today.

In fact, the number of skeptics may be growing. Their arguments can be found in books and sensational videos, such as a video called *Conspiracy Theory: Did We Land on the Moon?* There are countless conspiracy-based websites suggesting that the moon landing was faked.

But many knowledgeable scientists point out something important. All these materials seem to reflect poor critical thinking skills. For every notion the skeptics put forth, there is a valid counterargument that is based on facts. For example, many skeptics point to the American flag, which in one of the photos seems to be flapping in the wind. They argue that because space is a vacuum, and there is no wind in a vacuum, the fact that the flag seems to wave is evidence that the image—and thus the entire moon landing—was faked.

But the facts offer a simple, logical explanation: The flag assembly was designed with a collapsible horizontal crossbar, so it would stand unfurled in the zero-atmosphere

Though evidence disproves their claims, conspiracy theorists suggest that the ripples in the American flag mean that the moon landing was faked.

environment. But when the astronauts tried to extend the crossbar, it bent and didn't extend fully. This gave the flag a rippling effect, as if it really were flapping in a lunar breeze.

A massive amount of material in the public domain serves to debunk the skeptics' so-called proofs. And when

Aldrin and Armstrong left some scientific equipment on the moon to collect data for further study.

you consider this material, which explains in detail virtually every aspect of every Apollo mission, a question comes to mind: If this is all made up, why would so many people bother to fake it? As a matter of fact, hundreds of thousands of people were involved in designing and creating all of the objects used in the Apollo program, from the massive Saturn rockets to the spacecraft, land rovers, spacesuits, and tiniest bits of instrumentation. Thousands of others maintained and repaired the equipment and provided such services as fueling and ground transportation. Were all of them just fantasizing that they were at work all those years?

Leaving the Moon

When the two-man *Eagle* crew blasted off from the moon to rendezvous with the command module, *Columbia*, they had spent more than two and a half hours on the lunar surface. The *Eagle* ascent module carried a full tank of fuel for the return flight. The astronauts were also carrying a few items that hadn't been with them when they landed. They had a heap of moon rocks, of course. But, most interesting to ordinary people, they were also bringing back a lot of amazing photographic images and video footage.

At the same time, Armstrong and Aldrin left a few things behind. About 100 items—5,000 pounds (2,268 kg) of stuff—to be exact. Some of the things that stayed on the moon were for future use—various devices that would continue to monitor lunar conditions, for instance.

But to lighten their load and ensure an easier takeoff,

the astronauts also threw out a lot of things they no longer needed, including plain old garbage. Everything from space boots and the life-support backpacks to hammers, antennas, and lunar module armrests had to go. In the garbage category, bags of human waste and empty food containers were also discarded.

A major part of the famous Buzz Aldrin photo remained

Aldrin remarked that the surface of the moon was one of "magnificent desolation."

WE CAME IN PEACE

The plaque left on the moon recognizes the event as a global human achievement, not a national one.

Knowing that the landing portion of *Eagle* would stay on the moon, NASA thought ahead. Although the flag the astronauts raised was an American one, the ladder that was left behind includes a plaque that indicates the universality of the Apollo 11 mission. Its silver surface displays images of our planet's eastern and western hemispheres. Beneath the images is an inscription: "Here men from the planet Earth first set foot upon the moon. July 1969, A.D. We came in peace for all mankind."

THE EAGLE HAS LANDED—AGAIN

Although it did not remain on the moon, *Eagle*'s ascent module nevertheless did not return to Earth. After its rendezvous with *Columbia*, it was released into lunar orbit. Just before the Apollo 12 flight in November 1969, NASA noted that *Eagle* was still likely to be orbiting the moon, although it undoubtedly crash-landed on the lunar surface several months later. After Apollo 11, the lunar modules were targeted to crash-land in specific locations. The crash would create a "moonquake" that could then be studied.

The command modules for the Apollo flights did return to Earth. They splashed down in various locations in the Pacific Ocean. They were retrieved and today are available to view at museums around the United States and the world.

behind as well. This was *Eagle*'s landing module, which served as the launch pad for the return trip to *Columbia*. It may still be sitting on the moon. Who knows how long it will survive in the harsh conditions there? But it will always survive in the imagination of anyone familiar with the photograph in which it was featured so prominently.

The Buzz Aldrin image we know as AS11-40-5903 will remain one of the most powerful existing representations of the achievements of humankind. Because of its bizarre beauty, its symbolic significance, and its widespread recognition as a major cultural marker, it will continue to inspire people to achieve great things, and it will long outlive the era in which it came to be.

Neil Armstrong's image of Buzz Aldrin on the moon is photographic evidence of one of the great human achievements of all time.

Timeline

October 4, 1957

Soviet Union launches
Sputnik 1.

Soviet Union launches
Sputnik 2.

November 3, 1957

April 12, 1961

Soviet cosmonaut Yuri Gagarin
becomes the first man in space.

May 7, 1961

Astronaut Alan Shepard
becomes the first
American in space.

January 31, 1958

United States launches *Explorer 1*.

October 4, 1958

NASA begins operations.

September 13, 1959

Unmanned Soviet spacecraft *Luna 2* becomes the first vehicle to make impact on the moon.

June 3, 1965

Edward White becomes the first American to "walk" in space.

March 18, 1965

Soviet cosmonaut Alexei Leonov becomes the first person to "walk" in space.

April 3, 1966

Soviet *Luna 10* becomes the first spacecraft to orbit the moon.

Timeline

Apollo 7 mission sends the first live telecasts back to Earth from orbit.

October 1966

January 27, 1967

First manned Apollo mission ends in disaster on the launch pad when three astronauts die in a flash fire.

July 15, 1975

United States and Soviet Union launch the Apollo-Soyuz Test Project, the first manned international space station. It was the last Apollo mission.

January 28, 1986

U.S. space shuttle *Challenger* explodes after liftoff, killing all seven crew members.

December 21, 1968

U.S. launches Apollo 8, carrying the first human crew to orbit the moon.

July 20, 1969

Apollo 11 astronauts Neil Armstrong and Edwin "Buzz" Aldrin become the first people to walk on the lunar surface.

December 1972

Apollo 17 crew becomes the last Apollo team to journey to the moon.

February 1, 2003

Because of structural damage, space shuttle *Columbia* disintegrates as it re-enters Earth's atmosphere after 16 days in space; all seven crew members die.

July 2009

World celebrates the 40th anniversary of the Apollo 11 moon landing.

Glossary

cosmonaut: astronaut belonging to the Soviet or Russian space programs

desolate: empty, deserted

exposure: length of time that photographic film is exposed to light to make a picture

hoax: act of trickery or fakery

iconic: widely viewed as perfectly capturing the meaning or spirit of something or someone

lunar: of, relating to, or resembling the moon; designed for use on the moon

module: independently operable unit that is a part of the total structure of a space vehicle

photomontage: combination of photographic images

satellite: celestial or manmade object that orbits an object of a larger size, such as the moon or Earth

sovereignty: freedom from outside control; independence

treacherous: having hidden dangers

vacuum: space from which all air or gas has been emptied

Additional Resources

Further Reading

Aldrin, Buzz. *Look to the Stars*. New York: Putnam Juvenile, 2009.

Corrigan, Jim. *The 1960s Decade in Photos: Love, Freedom, and Flower Power*. Berkeley Heights, N.J.: Enslow Publishers, 2010.

Floca, Bryan. *Moon Shot: The Flight of Apollo 11*. New York: Atheneum/Richard Jackson Books, 2009.

Fradin, Dennis B. *First Lunar Landing*. New York: Marshall Cavendish Benchmark, 2010.

McPherson, Stephanie Sammartino. *The First Men on the Moon*. Minneapolis: Lerner Publications, 2009.

Platt, Richard. *Moon Landing*. Cambridge, Mass.: Candlewick, 2008.

Thimmesh, Catherine. *Team Moon: How 400,000 People Landed Apollo 11 on the Moon*. Boston: Houghton Mifflin, 2006.

Internet Sites

Use FactHound to find Internet sites related to this book. All of the sites on FactHound have been researched by our staff.

Here's all you do:
Visit *www.facthound.com*
Type in this code: 9780756543969

Source Notes

Page 4, line 19: Don E. Wilhelms. *To a Rocky Moon: A Geologist's History of Lunar Exploration.* Tucson: University of Arizona Press, 1993, p. 200.

Page 8, lines 2 and 4: Apollo Expedition to the Moon. NASA. 29 Oct. 2010. http://history.nasa.gov/SP-350/ch-11-4.html

Page 12, line 6: "July 20, 1969–One Giant Leap For Mankind." NASA. 29 Oct. 2010. www.nasa.gov/mission_pages/apollo/apollo11_40th.html

Page 16, line 3: John F. Kennedy. "Special Message to the Congress on Urgent National Needs." John F. Kennedy Presidential Library & Museum. 15 Oct. 2010. www.jfklibrary.org/Historical+Resources/Archives/Reference+Desk/Speeches/JFK/Urgent+National+Needs+Page+4.htm

Page 16, line 22: James Giglio. *The Presidency of John F. Kennedy.* Lawrence: University Press of Kansas, 1991, p.151.

Page 23, sidebar, line 28: James Oberg. *Uncovering Soviet Disasters.* New York: Random House, 1988, p. 156.

Page 30, sidebar, line 9: Tanja L. Zwan, ed. "Treaty on Principles Governing the Activities of States in the Exploration and Use of Outer Space, Including the Moon and Other Celestial Bodies of 27 January 1967." *Space Law: Views of the Future: A Compilation of Articles by a New Generation of Space Law Scholars.* Deventer, The Netherlands: Kluwer Law and Taxation Publishers, 1988, pp. 149–154.

Page 30, sidebar, lines 26 and 32: Anne M. Platoff. "Where No Flag Has Gone Before: Political and Technical Aspects of Placing a Flag on the Moon." NASA History Portal. 29 Oct. 2010. www.jsc.nasa.gov/history/flag/flag.htm

Page 38, lines 7 and 10: "From the Lunar Surface, a Message to Mission Control: The Eagle Has Landed." *The New York Times.* 21 July 1969, pp. 1–3.

Page 52, caption: Buzz Aldrin. *Magnificent Desolation: The Long Journey Home from the Moon.* New York: Random House, 2009, p. 34.

Page 53, sidebar, line 9: "The Apollo 11 Memorial on the Moon." High Energy Astrophysics Science Archive Research Center (HEASARC) at NASA. 29 Oct. 2010. http://starchild.gsfc.nasa.gov/docs/StarChild/space_level2/apollo11_plaque.html

Select Bibliography

Aldrin, Buzz. *Magnificent Desolation: The Long Journey Home from the Moon*. New York: Random House, 2009.

Apollo 11 Lunar Surface Journal. Corrected transcript and commentary by Eric M. Jones, 1995. 15 Oct. 2010. www.hq.nasa.gov/office/pao/History/alsj/a11/

Chalkin, Andrew. "Greatest Space Events of the 20th Century: The 60s." Space.com. 27 Dec. 1999. 15 Oct. 2010. www.space.com/news/spacehistory/greatest_space_events_1960s.html

"The Decision to Go to the Moon: President John F. Kennedy's May 25, 1961, Speech Before a Joint Session of Congress." NASA History Office. 15 Oct. 2010. http://history.nasa.gov/moondec.html

The First Lunar Landing: Introduction. NASA. 15 Oct. 2010. www.hq.nasa.gov/office/pao/History/ap11ann/FirstLunarLanding/ch-1.html

The First Lunar Landing: Part 1. NASA. 15 Oct. 2010. www.hq.nasa.gov/office/pao/History/ap11ann/FirstLunarLanding/ch-2.html

Ford, Matt. "Many small steps led to Apollo 11's giant leap for mankind." *Ars Technica*. 20 July 2009. 15 Oct. 2010. http://arstechnica.com/science/news/2009/07/many-small-steps-led-to-apollo-11s-giant-leap-for-mankind.ars/2

"From the Lunar Surface, a Message to Mission Control: The Eagle Has Landed." *The New York Times*. 21 July 1969, pp. 1–3.

Giglio, James N. *The Presidency of John F. Kennedy*. Lawrence: University Press of Kansas, 1991.

Griggs, Brandon. "Could moon landings have been faked? Some still think so." CNN.com. 17 July 2009. 15 Oct. 2010. www.cnn.com/2009/TECH/space/07/17/moon.landing.hoax/index.html

Kauffman, James L. *Selling Outer Space: Kennedy, the Media, and Funding for Project Apollo, 1961–1963*. Tuscaloosa: University of Alabama Press, 1994.

Logsdon, John M., and Alain Dupas. "Was the Race to the Moon Real?" *Scientific American*. Vol. 270 (June 1994), pp. 36–44.

"The Moon: A Giant Leap for Mankind." *Time*. 25 July 1969. 15 Oct. 2010. http://205.188.238.181/time/magazine/article/0,9171,901102-2,00.html

"The Moon: Awe, Hope and Skepticism on Planet Earth." *Time*. 25 July 1969. 15 Oct. 2010. http://205.188.238.181/time/magazine/article/0,9171,901105-1,00.html

Oberg, James. *Uncovering Soviet Disasters*. New York: Random House, 1988.

"On the Way Home From the Moon: A Conversation." *The New York Times*. 23 July 1969, p. 12.

"The (shady) story behind one of the most famous photos ever taken." Charles Apple. 15 Oct. 2010. www.visualeditors.com/apple/2009/03/the-shady-story-behind-one-of-the-most-famous-photos-ever-taken/

"Sputnik and the Dawn of the Space Age." Sputnik: The 50th Anniversary. NASA. 15 Oct. 2010. http://history.nasa.gov/sputnik/

Wilhelms, Don E. *To a Rocky Moon: A Geologist's History of Lunar Exploration*. Tucson: University of Arizona Press, 1993.

Index